At Home on a Coral Reef

by Ellen Sternhell

Modern Curriculum Press

Credits

Photos: All photos © Pearson Learning unless otherwise noted.

Front cover: Beverly Factor/International Stock. Title page: E.R. Degginger/Color-Pic, Inc. 5: Peter/Stef Lamberti/Tony Stone Images. 6–7: A. Witte/C. Mahaney/Tony Stone Images. 8: Mike Bacon/Tom Stack & Associates. 9: E.R. Degginger/Color-Pic, Inc. 10: Marc Chamberlain/Tony Stone Images. 11: Dave Fleetham/Tom Stack & Associates. 12: E.R. Degginger/Color-Pic, Inc. 13: Marty Snyderman/WaterHouse Stock. 14: Stephen Frink/Tony Stone Images. 15: Kenneth J. Howard/Sea Images. 16: Uniphoto Picture Agency. 17: l. Stephen Frink, r. Bill Harrigan/WaterHouse Stock. 18–19: ©Andrew J. Martinez/Photo Researchers, Inc. 20: Jeff Rotman. 21: E.R. Degginger/Color-Pic, Inc. 22: Stuart Westmorland/Westmorland Photography. 23: E.R. Degginger/Animals Animals. 24: l. Phil Degginger, r. E.R. Degginger/Color-Pic, Inc. 25: ©Fred Winner/Jacana/Photo Researchers, Inc. 26: E.R. Degginger/Color-Pic, Inc. 27: Bill Harrigan/WaterHouse Stock. 28: Dave Fleetham/Tom Stack & Associates. 29: Jeff Rotman. 30: Fred Bavendam/Peter Arnold, Inc. 31: Stephen Frink/WaterHouse Stock.

Cover and book design by Lisa Ann Arcuri

ISBN 0–7652–1363-X

Printed in the United States of America

14 15   10 09

Modern Curriculum Press

Pearson Learning Group

1-800-321-3106
www.pearsonlearning.com

Contents

To Brandon and Tyler, who are just
beginning to discover the beauty and
wonder of the world!

What Is a Coral Reef?

The earth is made of land and water. Many plants and animals live on the land. Other plants and animals live in the water.

There are places where the water is not too deep. One of these places is a coral reef. Many fish and other sea animals live there.

Coral colors are bright.

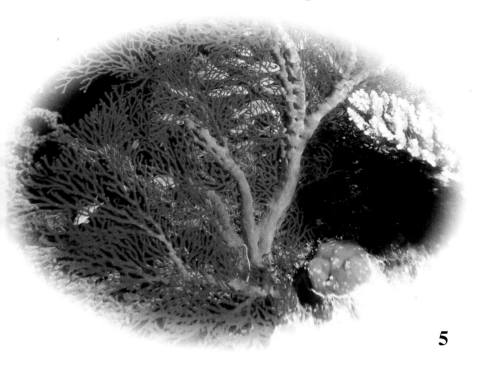

A reef is a strip of sand or rock under the water. A coral reef is a different kind of reef. It is made of tiny animals that live close together. These animals are called corals.

Corals need warm water and sunlight to live. So you will find corals where the water is not too deep. Here the sun warms the water.

A diver explores a coral reef.

It takes many years to build a coral reef. After corals die, their hard shells remain. New corals grow on top of the old shells.

After a long time the corals pile up. The reef begins to look like rock. The coral would feel sharp if you touched it.

What does one coral look like? Look at the picture below. A hard shell grows around the coral's soft body. The shell is shaped like a cup.

You can see the coral's mouth in the picture. The long things that grow around the mouth are called tentacles. A coral uses its tentacles to catch food.

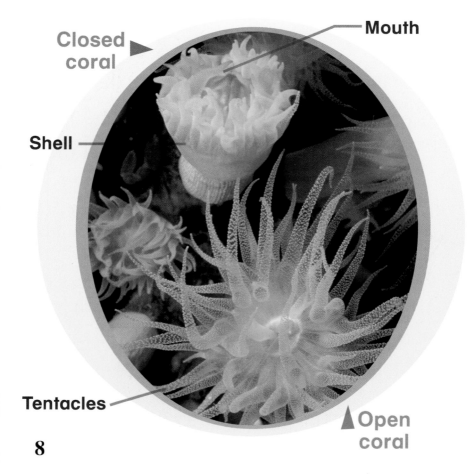

Closed coral

Mouth

Shell

Tentacles

Open coral

8

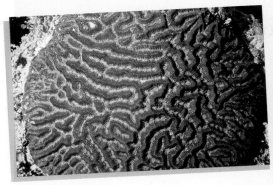

▲ **Brain coral**

Sea pen coral ▶

Many corals have been named for their shapes. Look at the pictures above. What does each shape look like to you?

Reef ☆ Fact

Corals eat tiny fish and other animals. They cannot move to find food. The moving water carries food to them.

Chapter 2
Colorful Fish

A coral reef is a busy home under the sea. Many colorful fish live there.

Angelfish have spots and lines on their bodies. These patterns make it hard for bigger fish to see them.

Emperor angelfish by coral

Baby angelfish

Baby angelfish are dark blue with white rings. These colors help to hide the little fish.

Angelfish also have flat bodies. They can swim easily in and out of the coral. They eat tiny plants and animals that live on the reef.

Mandarin fish

The mandarin fish is another colorful reef fish. It hides in cracks at the bottom of the reef. It waits to catch and eat smaller fish that swim by.

The mandarin fish has thick skin. Its skin smells and tastes bad. The bad taste keeps large fish away. They don't want to eat the mandarin.

Harlequin tusk fish

The tusk fish is a reef fish with something different. It is named for the four blue teeth that stick out of its mouth. The tusk fish uses its teeth to turn things over. The teeth help the fish catch any food it finds.

Reef ☆ Fact

More than 2,000 kinds of fish have been found in a coral reef.

The Sea Horse

One coral reef fish does not look like a fish. It has a head like that of a horse. It has a tail like that of a monkey. It has a pouch like that of a kangaroo. It is called a sea horse.

Sea horse

The sea horse has a head shaped like
a horse's head.

A sea horse looks a little like a horse. This is
because of its mouth. The mouth is a long tube.
The tube is like a drinking straw. It helps the sea
horse take in food.

15

The sea horse cannot swim very fast.
So it hooks its tail around the coral. It waits
for food to pass by.

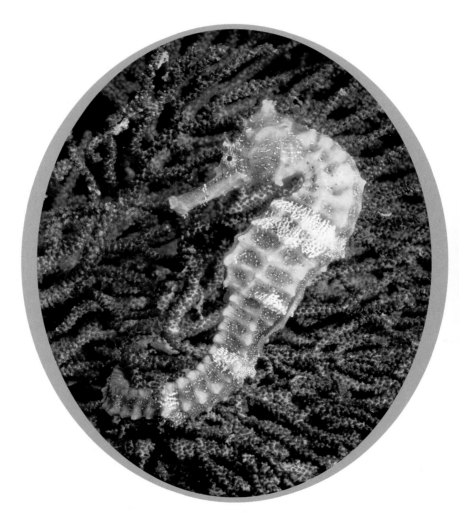

Sea horse wrapped around coral

The sea horse uses its fins and tail to move. It straightens its tail to go up. It curls its tail to go down.

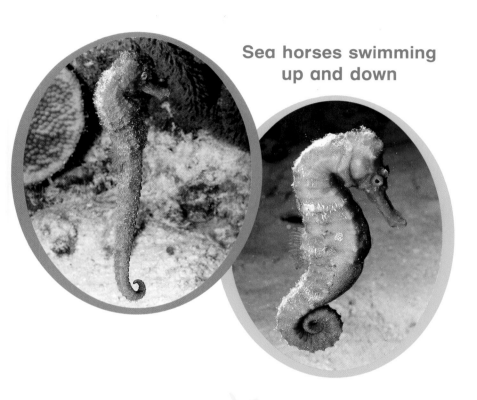

Sea horses swimming up and down

Reef ☆ Fact

The sea horse can move each eye a different way. It can see two things at the same time.

Chapter 4

An Animal That Looks Like a Plant

Some coral reef animals look like plants. The sea anemone is an animal that looks like a flower. Its name sounds something like "uh NEM uh nee."

On top of the anemone are tentacles. They look like spikes. These tentacles have a poison in them. The poison can sting. The tentacles sting small fish that swim too close. Then the anemone eats the fish.

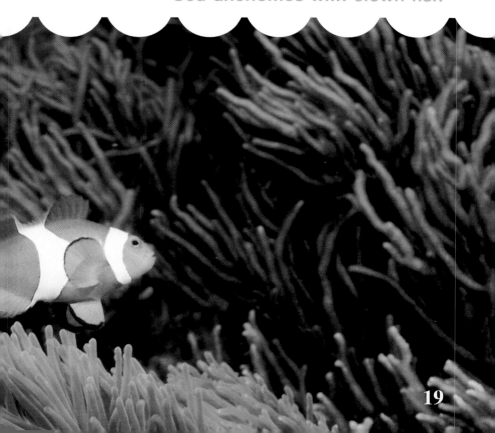

Sea anenomes with clown fish

The clown fish is not hurt by the sea anemone. The clown fish and the sea anemone help each other. The clown fish hides from enemies in the anemone's tentacles. Some fish may want to eat the anemone. Then the clown fish comes out. It chases away the other fish.

Pink clown fish

Hermit crab with sea anemones

The anemone also helps the hermit crab. Sometimes a crab sticks an anemone onto its shell. The anemone stings animals that try to eat the crab.

Reef ☆ Fact

The hermit crab lives in a shell. It is a shell that another animal has left. The crab looks for bigger shells to move into as it grows.

Starfish and Clams

Some clams make their home on a coral reef. All baby clams are small. Many adult clams never grow bigger than your hand.

Giant clam with shell partly opened

Giant clam with shell partly closed

The giant clam grows to be very big. It is also too heavy to pick up. It weighs up to 500 pounds.

The shell of a clam has two parts. The clam opens its shell to eat, then closes it tight. The clam's soft body is safe inside the hard shell.

A clam's shell is hard to open when it is closed. There is one animal that can open a clam's shell. That animal is the starfish.

Look at the shape of a starfish. You can see how it got its name. The points of the starfish are called arms. All starfish have at least five arms. Some have more than five arms.

Starfish come in many colors.

The starfish stretches its arms across the clam's shell. Little suckers on the starfish's arms stick to the clam's shell. Then the arms start to pull. It can take hours to open the shell. Finally the shell is open a little. Then the starfish can get in to eat the clam.

A starfish opening a clam

The underside of a starfish

Look at the picture of the underside of a starfish. On the arms you can see the suckers. The starfish uses these to open the clam. The mouth is in the middle of the body.

There are many different kinds of starfish. The crown-of-thorns starfish is a danger to the reef. It kills the coral by eating it.

Crown-of-thorns starfish

Reef ☆ Fact

Sometimes a starfish loses an arm. Then the starfish grows a new one.

Chapter 6
The Octopus

Another animal that lives around the coral reef also has many arms. This animal is the octopus. It has eight arms.

Octopus

Suckers on an octopus arm

The octopus is like the starfish. It also has suckers on its arms. The suckers help the octopus hold onto rocks and food.

The coral reef is a good place for the octopus. Its soft body can hide in little cracks in the reef. There the octopus is safe.

An octopus can also change colors. It will change colors to look like the place where it hides. An octopus can be brown and blue. It can also be white, yellow, orange, or green.

An octopus can change its shape, too. It can be long and thin to move quickly. It can be big and round to look scary.

An octopus can also shoot black ink out of its body. The ink makes a dark cloud. Then an enemy can't see the octopus swim away.

Octopus shooting out ink

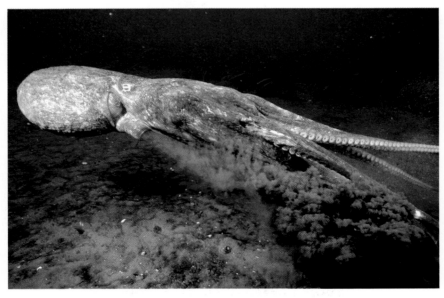

Broken elkhorn coral

Many coral reefs and the animals that live there are in danger. People break off pieces with their boats. They kill the reefs by dumping garbage in the water. People need to find ways to help save the reefs before they are gone.

Reef ☆ Fact

Sometimes a coral reef grows out of the water. Then it becomes an island. People can live on the island.

Glossary

enemies [EH nuh meez] any things that harm

garbage [GAHR bihj] things that are thrown away

hook [hook] hang onto

island [EYE lund] land with water all around it

pouch [powch] a part of the belly of an animal that is like a pocket

shell [shel] the hard outer part of some animal

sucker [SUH kur] a part of an animal used for taking food into the mouth or for hanging onto something

tentacle [TEN tih kul] a long, thin part of some animals that grows around the head or the mouth